IT TAKES A FOOL

A Tough Lesson Learned On Bullying

SASHA DREAMS

Cover Art by Xuyinyin

IT TAKES A FOOL

Copyright © 2014 by I Dream Business, LLC

All rights reserved. This book or any portion thereof may not be reproduced or used in any manner whatsoever without the express written permission of the publisher except for the use of brief quotations in a book review.

This story is copyrighted under the United States Copyright Office. Any infringement of this story will lead to legal action.

For my ancestors, who come to me in my dreams to remind me of my worth.

A CREATIVE MEMOIRE

"Once you begin to write the true story of your life in a form that anyone would possibly want to read, you start to make compromises with the truth."

- Ben Yagoda

Before destruction a person's heart is proud, but humility comes before honor. *Please God, consider me humbled...*

- Proverbs 18:12

ACKNOWLEDGEMENTS

The disciples came to Jesus in private and asked, "why couldn't we drive it out?" He replied, "because you have so little faith. Truly I tell you, if you have the faith as small as a mustard seed, you can say to the mountain, 'move from here to there,' and it will move. Nothing will be impossible for you."

- Matthew 17:19-20

Self-publishing is full of many mountains. I am eternally grateful to all of you who helped me move them all.

To my husband: how can I express my gratitude? You held my hand, you pushed, you challenged, you listened, and you stood by my side, word for word. I am in love with you.

My beautiful, caring and kind three sons. Thank you for your input, love, and encouraging words. I love you.

To my sisters: I am so proud of you all. Thank you for loving me in spite of me. Love you ladies.

Mom and Dad, we have been through the fire but we were not singed. God is good!

To my friends and coworkers, who suggested, commented, and supported me every step of the way. Thank you.

To the elegant ladies of Turning Pages: thank you for your friendship, love, prayers and support.

To Angenette Alexander-Smith, Jernell Brown, Daniel B. Cooper 3, Jalyn Ely, J. Kelly, Xuyinyin, Cherrail Curry, Eon L. Lewis, and everyone else who made this book come to life: Thank you.

Dear Reader,

You don't know my story, and neither do I, for I have blocked a great deal of it out in order to function "normally." Bear with me as I attempt to unlock the inner depths of my soul and unshackle my inner child to let her finally have a voice.

The child I've managed to suppress for more than twenty-five years is a ten-year-old "brown" girl named Sasha. She was four feet tall, with natural brown hair and large brown eyes. Slim yet muscular. Cute, not beautiful. From the beginning, her parents said, "She's been here before." Her first words being "Kurtis Blow" all but confirmed this theory. Sasha transitioned into gifted and talented classes in the first grade. Besides the love of listening to music, reading Encyclopedia Britannica was one of her favorite pastimes.

Throughout this story, you may find yourself feeling animosity toward her. You may know her or someone like her. You may be her. When or if these feelings occur, I ask that you close your eyes, go to a quiet place in your mind, and try not to judge her. Instead, pray for her. Pray for you or the girl you know who is like her. After you have prayed, have peace and know that God is still God.

I learned much later in life that freedom is not free. My prayer is that you will accept my apology. Hold on to your seats and ride this emotional roller coaster with me...

PART 1

Dear Sadie,

This is an attempt to apologize for the wrongs I've done to you. I now know that I only hurt you because I was hurt. Interestingly enough, I come from a long line of ancestral hurt, betrayal, emptiness, broken promises, enslavement (mental and physical), insecurities, and lack. Bullying was the path I chose to handle the hurt. A path that in turn came back to bite me with a force that has to be out of this world. The universe gave me what I chose to give to you. Please understand that nothing I say is in any way justification for my actions, because nothing I say can excuse them. This is only an attempt to share my story with you so that we, or maybe just me, can be set free.

The year was 1989. I was ten years old and felt like life was just beginning. My family brought the year in with a bang. Just the year before, my parents had scored major positions with the companies they worked for, and we moved into a luxurious townhouse in the suburbs.

If I remember correctly, this was how Mom described it to her girlfriends: "Yes, girl, it's beautiful! Three entire finished levels, plush carpet throughout. A huge gourmet kitchen with top-of-the-line appliances from Sears. Three oversized bedrooms, a large deck, and a spacious back yard. My husband just loves me."

My mother was doing data entry for Dun and Bradstreet. She was promoted to project manager, but only agreed to accept the position if she could be home when I came in from school.

In the beginning, coming home from school was one of the best parts of my day. Mom would be waiting for me in the kitchen. She would have a plate of fresh sliced peaches and a tall glass of orange juice. Mom would want to hear the full details of my day. "Good" wasn't good enough for Mom.

I remember her standing in the kitchen. She was beautiful. She stood about five feet five inches tall, and had a warm caramel complexion. She used to rock a blown-out afro, but since her promotion, she told the girls at the salon we frequented every Tuesday to give her a press and curl. Mom had huge brown eyes that glowed like the moon when she smiled, which made you want to smile, too. She had a slim waist and a clothing style she ordered from Bloomingdale's.

I would hang out in the kitchen with Mom and watch her prepare dinner. I always hoped that one day I would be as good a cook as she was. The fuzz from the sliced peaches would tickle my tongue as I recounted my day. Taking my time to retell every last detail so I would be the first to hear the jingle of Dad's keys as he unlocked the front door.

My dad was a computer engineer for a major telecommunications company called MCI. He had just been promoted to supervisor of his team. Dad was five feet seven inches tall, athletically built, with dark brown skin. His afro was medium length and neatly trimmed. The only time you would catch him out of his tailor-made suits with Cool Water cologne was when he was on the basketball court.

When I heard the key in the door, I'd run and hide behind the couch. Dad would say, "Hello, family," and I would take off running into his arms. Dad would pick me up and throw me high into the air. He would spin me round and round until we were both dizzy with love.

Mom would wait patiently in the doorway of the kitchen for her turn with Dad. He would rush into Mom's open arms. They would hug, kiss and stare into each other's eyes. They would share intimate details of their day in a language I could only interpret as love.

If only the good times could have outnumbered the bad.

I also had a little sister. Her name was Sarah. She had just turned four that year and was starting to be a pain in my you-know-what.

Back then, I didn't know much about the companies they worked for. I did know that whatever they were, they were big and super rich. Company parties were how we spent our weekends. Pools, hotels, yachts. If none of these lavish parties were happening, then our house was the designated party house. People were always coming and going.

It seemed that in such a short amount of time, money became a non-issue for us. I'll never forget the day that Dad, on a whim, decided to buy a 1989 Cadillac Seville. As soon as we drove the brand-spanking-new car off the lot, Dad popped in his favorite tape. The Spinners. *Rubberband Man* blasted on the new stereo system.

That's when the lights and sirens started wailing behind us. My dad pulled over and turned the music off.

The officer came halfway to the car and ordered him out of the vehicle.

From the back seat and peering out of the window, I heard the officer demanding, "Whose car is this?"

"It's mine," my dad started to explain. Next thing I knew, the officer pulled out his gun and ordered Dad to the ground.

"What's the bulge in your front pocket?" the officer screamed. I could barely hear Dad at that point. He sounded humiliated, angry, and another emotion I couldn't pinpoint.

"It's money," I finally heard Dad say. The officer told Dad to "slowly reach into your jacket pocket and produce the weapon."

Weapon? What weapon? I wondered.

Dad reached into his pocket and pulled out a large wad of money. "What are you, a drug dealer?" the cop asked.

"No, I just cashed my check. I was going to use it as a down payment for this car, but—"

The cop rudely cut off my dad's explanation. "I'm going to need to see some proof of this, boy."

Boy? I wondered.

Dad was allowed to get off the ground and come back to the car. The officer continued to point his gun at Dad. Dad looked cool, calm, and collected, but his hands shook as he showed the officer his pay receipt. "I was trying to tell you, I work for MCI. I brought this money to use as a down payment, but the guy at the dealership said my credit was so high, I didn't need one."

The officer lowered his weapon. A look of shame and a bit of jealousy crossed his face. He tried to make small talk about satellites, but Dad was uninterested at that point. I guess the officer noticed his agitation. He apologized for the misunderstanding and told Dad that he was free to go.

The rest of the way home, Dad went on and on about how white people weren't used to seeing black people with anything. Eventually, he changed beats, saying he was not going to let that "pig" ruin his night. We were having another party. He turned his beloved Spinners back on and zoned out. I went into a zone myself, wondering for the first time if what the "pig" had said was true.

Was my dad a drug dealer?

My mind went back to all the drugs I had sneakingly seen people doing at the company parties. Things I saw people sniffing and drinking. The colorful drinks with fruit that looked like they tasted so good. Things I wasn't allowed to have. Not even a sip. When I asked Mom what everything was, she told me it was "grown folks' candy".

I knew better than that because of DARE, the Drug Abuse Resistance Education program, at school. If Dad was a drug dealer, then Mom must know about it.

Were we in trouble? So many questions swam through my mind, but I couldn't give them any more thought. We were having another house party that night.

I knew all too well what that meant. Lots of my parents' friends, co-workers and their kids were coming over. They would eat, play cards, laugh, dance, and listen to my father's record collection, and there was going to be plenty of "grown folks' candy." All of us kids would be ordered to stay up in my bedroom. We were given movies such as *Nightmare On Elm Street* (parts one through four), plates of food, soda pop, and strict instruction not to leave the room for any reason.

This gave lots of opportunity for me and the boys to frequent my closet and dry hump. We would lay on top of my rows upon rows of shoes and grind on each other. I remember liking it when the boys got on top of me. We would make funny noises and press our private areas on each other through our jeans. We stayed in there until one of the parents came to check on us. They would snatch us out of the closet and tell us to stop being nasty. I didn't understand what that meant, because we were just copying what the people did in the R-rated movies we were watching.

The day after these house parties was always the worst for me. I took on the responsibility of cleaning up because I wanted the house to return to normal as quickly as possible. I never wanted my little sister to see what I saw. I'd come downstairs the following morning to what I referred to as the "morning-after song." The Spinners were always on my father's record player and without fail, *"Love Don't Love Nobody (It Takes A Fool)"* would be stuck on repeat. I'd walk into the smoke-filled living room to naked parents. Naked parents, friends and co-workers. The house would be trashed. Beer cans strewn all over, empty plates of food. Burnt cigarettes overflowed the ashtrays. Candle wax laid melted on our beautiful cherry wood tables. Dad's prized albums, Kool and the Gang, The Stylistics, Kurtis Blow, Prince, Michael Jackson, laid face down in milk crates, just waiting to be scratched.

What bothered me most was that the framed family photos were always off the bookshelves. They would be scattered around the house. One in the kitchen, one in the living room, the bathroom, various locations around the house, but all covered in white powder. Traces of "grown folks' candy" left behind from the night before.

I always took my time cleaning my fifth-grade school picture. I loved that picture of me. It was the first time I considered myself anything other than cute. I seemed to have a glow. I wore a dress that my aunt sent. It was purple and green--my favorite colors. My mother cornrowed my shoulder-length natural hair in two long braids and tied purple and green ribbons at the end. I considered hiding that picture so my parents and their friends would no longer cut up their "candy" on my face, but I kept feeling like if one picture was out of place, I'd never be able to return our home back to normal.

So I quietly went around covering my parents' nakedness and waking up their friends. It usually didn't take much coaxing to get them to leave. Just the sight of me was usually enough to have them scrambling for the door. I tried not to let the parties or their aftermath get me down. I looked forward to my parents waking up sometime that afternoon and taking me and Sarah to the park. Oh, how I remember the smell of the honeysuckles that greeted us as we got out of the car! We would fly kites, ride bikes, and laugh and play until the sun went to light the other side of the world. That's what I focused on while I cleaned up the the terrors of the night.

Monday mornings were such a welcome treat. My elementary school, a massive one-story brown brick building that was full of color and light, was my getaway. A safe haven from the roller coaster ride at home. I actually enjoyed learning. It came easily, and I loved the attention from teachers for my good work. Even more than the learning and the attention, I couldn't wait to get to school to see Sadie. No matter what mood I was in on Monday morning, just seeing Sadie made the day brighter.

Sadie was "Caucasian", four feet tall like me, athletic, long blond hair with blue eyes and two freckles on both sides of her cheeks. She was beautiful. Sadie was always happy. If anyone was feeling blue, Sadie had the words to turn their frown upside down. She was my friend from the moment we met, my ace boon coon. We were two peas in a pod and all the other clichés. You couldn't tell us we did not run the fifth grade. Whenever you saw Sadie, you saw me, and vice versa. We were inseparable.

The two things we definitely owned at our school were spelling bees and kickball. No one older, male or female, could beat us at either game. We would study words at lunch and challenge new teams to kickball during recess. It got to a point where Sadie and I would play two against four or five. We were that doggone good.

The latest hype we had going was Sadie's slumber party for her eleventh birthday. It was all we talked about for weeks. Who should "we" invite, what matching dresses we were going to wear. How we were going to wear our hair and how we were going to convince our mothers to let us wear makeup and heels. With all the excitement, it was hard for me to understand the look of fear or worry I sometimes saw in Sadie's eyes. This was the only time I saw her in a light other than pure joy.

We were finally able to narrow the invite list down to eight girls. Sadie's mom said that Sadie could invite as many girls as she wanted, but "we" thought it best to keep it exclusive. I didn't want to share Sadie with too many people. Anyway, this was going to be my first opportunity to spend time with the family that she spoke so highly of. Our parents apparently didn't believe in "playdates". There was always an excuse as to why we couldn't hang out on the weekends. Besides that, her parents sounded like picture-perfect people.

Nothing like my parents. At any given moment, they would, as it seemed, break up just to make up. One minute they loved each other; the next, they couldn't stand each other's guts. Somehow, my little sister Sarah remained their "little princess" through all the ups and downs.

Sadie never complained about her little sister. She never told stories like mine, where I felt like recently my parents loved Sarah more than me. How Dad sometimes looked at Sarah like she was his firstborn. How she was able to go joyriding with him and I got told to "stay home and help Mom clean," and how that really meant that Mom watched soap operas while I cleaned the house.

Sadie never had explanations like mine about why she missed a week of school. Like when Dad slapped Mom. Mom would get mad, and there would be a lot of screaming and cursing. Always, the same few belongings thrown in the same suitcase. Always, the eight-hour drive to Grandmother's house. Always, Mom vowing to be done with Dad's bullshit. Always, Grandmother telling Mom that husbands slap their wives: "That's how they gain control." Grandmother continually telling Mom that she couldn't keep running away every time Dad put his hands on her. Always, five days later, Mom driving us back home with open arms for Dad, just in time for another house party. Sadie's family sounded nothing like mine.

The weeks before Sadie's party were life-changing at home. There was talk of things I hadn't heard of before. Layoffs, job cuts, companies going belly-up, late mortgage payments, missing money, addiction, foreclosure, abortion. Mom and Dad were constantly at each other's throats. Dad spent a lot of nights away from home. Mom stayed up all night crying. She wouldn't cook for me and Sarah on those nights. I was left to fend for the both of us. Mom would lay on the couch and cry as I opened cans of vegetables and fed them to Sarah.

I tried my best to keep things in order. I did the laundry that piled up. I vacuumed, I washed my mom's face while she slept. All the while hoping that if things appeared to be perfect at home, Dad would come back.

And eventually, he did. Two to three days later, begging Mom to forgive him for his addiction. He promised he would stop doing drugs, and he was sorry but he had spent all of his savings while he was gone. Mom told Dad that she would forgive him as long as he promised to stop this addiction, because she was going to have this baby.

I watched in silence as my father cried and promised to do better. Something inside of me broke that day. It wasn't until much later that I'd find out what it was.

Dad brought home an all-white kitten after this escapade. While the kitten was the cutest thing I had ever seen, all I could think was now I would have a new baby and a new kitten to take care of.

The following weeks brought in the full clarity of our situation. Mom and Dad stopped going to work. When I finally asked why, Mom explained that they had been laid off.

"Laid off?" I asked.

"Yes," she explained. Dad's company was starting to lose business to other telecommunication companies and needed to cut back on their employees. Mom's job was relocating, and the office only needed one project manager at the new location. Somehow, Mom was not the one they needed. She went on to say that Dad had to find a new job soon or we were going to lose everything.

Suddenly, the reality of our situation became so dark for me. Mom stopped getting off the couch. Dad stayed away for longer periods of time. The kitten, who my father named Snow, became ill and stopped eating. Sarah made every effort to feed the cat by putting a trail of cat food across every square inch of the house.

Things rapidly fell apart. I couldn't keep up with the long list of responsibilities. I looked around at the mayhem that had become our lives. I found myself longing for the days of the house and company parties. I ached for the days when Dad would rush home to see Mom and tell her about his day. The way he seemed to melt whenever she was near. I missed the laughter. Their intimate touches and their lingering kisses. I missed spa days with Mom, where she would tell me she had to stay "fly" for Dad. My skin craved the feeling of the sun from the long hours at the park. I even missed the jealousy I felt when my parents' world would stand still at any microscopic normal gesture Sarah made. They used to look at her with so much love. Now, she could eat cat food, and no one would notice.

I missed those days so badly it hurt. Where did the love go? Did the drugs take away the love too? Did the layoff? Where did it all go? I needed to find it. I had to restore our home.

Then as if someone had slapped me across the face, I realized, *"It takes a fool to learn that love don't love nobody."*

That realization actually made the day-to-day routine more bearable. I decided to focus back on the things that used to make me happy. In addition to Sadie's slumber party coming that Saturday, I also had a DARE Spelling Bee competition Friday.

I only had one week to find the perfect gift for Sadie, something that would light her back up like the Sadie she used to be. With all the commotion at home, it was harder for me to pinpoint what exactly was wrong with Sadie. She looked like she was losing weight and appeared tired all the time. She no longer wanted to play kickball at recess. She would say, "I'm tired, we beat them already, it looks like rain, I can't get these shoes dirty." She had one excuse after another. I had to put Sadie's lack of interest in kickball on the back burner and focus on the spelling bee.

The school gave us a list of more than 300 words that pertained to drug and substance abuse. Go figure. So many words on the list were being thrown around at home on a daily basis. I was more than ready for this bee. Good thing, too, because the winner of this competition would compete in the Augustus County spelling bee. How wonderful it would be to win. First prize was $1,000. Maybe that would be enough money to pay the mortgage. Maybe that would be enough for Dad to come home and say, "Hello, family," again. Maybe he wouldn't feel the need to stay away so often. Maybe it would be enough to make my parents be able to see me again. Maybe, just maybe.

That week of school seemed to fly by. Sadie and I had worked out all the details of the party. I managed to convince her to wear a purple and green dress. I knew I couldn't get Mom to buy me a new dress now. I had a few other loose ends to tie up before Saturday. I still had to get a birthday gift for Sadie, and I had to make sure home was going to be okay without me for the night. I managed to arrange for Jennifer, a girl down the street who was also invited, to ask her mom to give me a ride to the party. I couldn't count on mine to be in a mood for driving. I also needed to make sure there was enough food in the house for Sarah.

Thursday after school, I decided to venture pass my knowledge of cooking. I would make a real dinner. That way, Sarah could eat the leftovers while I was at Sadie's.

That evening, I was able to convince Mom to give me a ride to the grocery store to buy food. We pulled up to Walmart. I remember Mom saying she liked the new Walmart concept because you could get everything you needed under one roof. Everything? Hopefully Sadie's special gift was included in that everything.

Mom gave me what cash she had and told me that her and Sarah would wait in the car. I tried to buy the things I had seen Mom buy so many times in the past, and also things that didn't require much cooking. I remember getting to the checkout counter and seeing the bracelets. They were silver, with a charm heart that was intentionally broken in two. One part of the charm said "best" and the other said "friends." No way could I afford them, so I hurriedly put the bracelets in my pocket before anyone could see me.

I nervously left the store, looking over my shoulder the entire time. It wasn't until the groceries were in the trunk and Mom drove out of the parking lot that I was able to breathe.

That night, I decided to fry chicken like I had seen Mom do countless times before. I decorated the chicken with all the seasonings in the cabinet until it looked like the raw chicken I used to sneakily lick. I put oil in the pan and turned on the gas. I let the grease sizzle, floured the chicken in a plastic Ziploc bag and shook it with all my might. I fried that chicken! I even made some Rice-a-Roni with broccoli. The house smelled delicious. It was the first meal we'd had in a very long time. I set the table in the formal dining room and used Mom's good china from the china cabinet. I was able to persuade Mom to join Sarah and me at the table. What a treat. It was as if God had shone his light down on us at that moment, and because of the light we were able to smile.

Lo and behold, as if on cue, Dad walked through the door. After the commotion of welcoming him back home, even though he smelled badly and his hair and clothes were unkempt, we ate, we laughed, and we conversed as if we hadn't skipped a beat.

At some point during the meal, Sarah started to point to the kitchen and say, "Fire". I thought it was another lame attempt for her to get attention, but no, there was a fire, a huge fire. Suddenly, I remembered that I forgot to turn off the pan of grease.

"Oh no! The grease!" I screamed.

Dad rushed into the kitchen to extinguish the fire with all of the water he could get from the sink. Me, Mom, and Sarah watched from the far end of the dining room in fear. If Dad had of been himself, he would have remembered that you don't fight a grease fire with water. But given what may, this father, or what was left of him, continued to throw water even as the flames grew stronger.

Luckily, the neighbors saw the smoke coming from the back porch and called 911. The fire department was there in no time. Only the kitchen had been destroyed. The rest of the house was deemed safe.

My mother did provide me with some comfort that night. She came to my bedroom to tuck me in. She sat at the foot of my bed, not saying anything for a long while. Eventually, she told me that the fire wasn't my fault, and that all in all, it was still a good dinner.

I did not sleep easy that night. My parents shouts grew louder and louder. I climbed out of bed and crept through the shadowy hallways. I sat at the top of the dark and lonely staircase, listening in on the argument. Mom kept asking Dad where he had been, and Dad was yelling that of course he couldn't stay home with us now because we didn't have a kitchen.

Even though the night had been a disaster, I woke up the following morning excited for the future. I decided not to let my yesterday dictate my today. Today was the day I would win the spelling bee that would save my family. I jumped out of bed and picked out a cute green shirt and my favorite stonewashed blue jeans. I took my time brushing my hair, had to be ready to pose for the pictures. I grabbed Sadie's half of the charm bracelet. I wanted to be the first person to give her a birthday gift. *"I'll find the perfect time today to surprise her,"* I thought. I ran downstairs and choked on the smoke from the kitchen, but was able to remind Mom not to be late for the spelling bee that started at three o' clock.

"I'll be there," she said without looking at me.

The school day flew by. I stayed focused on my list of words. I didn't study with Sadie at lunch like we usually did. Instead, I took the list into the girls' bathroom and went over them alone. I stared at the pink bathroom stall walls, trying to make heads or tails of where my family was headed. The longer I stared, the more clearly I could see the writing on the wall. Hallucinogens, amphetamines, cannabis, cocaine, the list went on and on. Visions of the drugs, the arguing, and Dad's rapidly deteriorating health suddenly made it impossible to remain focused.

The next thing I knew, I was in the auditorium, sitting on stage, looking out into the audience. There were approximately twenty-five people in the crowd, but no sign of Mom and Sarah. I looked to the left of me and saw a row of empty chairs. To the right was Sadie.

A woman down in the audience was speaking into a microphone. "Sasha, you have thirty seconds to respond or you will be disqualified. Sasha, the last word of the day is 'addiction.' Whoever spells this word correctly will qualify to be in the Agustus County spelling bee championship."

I stood and walked over to the microphone on stage. I looked again in the crowd for Mom. *Mom, where are you? I need you here*, I thought.

Suddenly, in my mind's eye, I saw Mom. She was standing in our living room. She was crying, and Dad was there too.

"Mom, Dad, can you hear me? I need you to come to my school for the spelling bee."

Mom continued to cry. "Honey, I need you here with us. The girls need you here with us. We need you to be the husband and father that you used to be. Stay here with us, and we will get you some help. Stop this addiction and choose your family," Mom begged.

Dad stared at Mom, and for a second it seemed he was going to take her into his arms, but something,

something bigger than his love for her, made him say, "I don't need this shit! I don't need you, I don't need the girls, and I don't have a problem that I need help with. I'll come home when you get off my fucking back about it." Dad stormed out the front door, and Mom fell to her knees.

"Sasha, this is your final call. The word is addiction."

I cleared my throat, and in a small voice I spelled, "D-A-D-D-Y."

"That is incorrect," the woman said in disbelief. The woman then called Sadie to the stage. "The word is addiction."

Sadie slowly walked to the microphone, keeping her eyes on me the entire time.

I stared straight past Sadie, trying to avoid any and all eye contact. I stared into my dark future. I had lost all hope to restore the love that was lost for my family. *Love, love, love, stop making a fool of me.* The walls closed in on me. The room went dark, but I was still able to see that the audience had all turned into jokers. They laughed and pointed. "Fool," I heard them say.

Through the hallucinations, I heard Sadie as she whispered into the microphone, "A-D-D-I-C-T-I-O-N, sorry, Sasha"

The lights grew bright and in a cheery voice the woman said: "And that makes Sadie the winner."

The room burst into applause. I took Sadie's charm bracelet from my front jean pocket. "Congratulations," I said and shoved the bracelet into her hands before I ran, crying, hurt, and humiliated, from the auditorium. Devastated. I was not able to save my family.

Sleep did not find me that night. I lay in bed for hours tossing and turning. At some point the following day, a knock sounded at the front door. *Shit, it must be Jennifer.* I rolled out of bed and grabbed my purple and green dress out of the dirty clothes hamper. Not bothering to iron or brush hair or teeth, I walked out of the house dazed, "ready" to go. Not even bothering to tell Mom or Sarah that I was leaving for the night. Jennifer and her mom asked me several times if everything was okay. Her mom even offered me a brush. I didn't respond. I just stared out of the car window the entire ride.

As we pulled up to Sadie's house, I was in awe. Sadie's single-family home was three times the size of our townhouse. There were servants outside dressed in black and white, eager to greet and welcome us to "Sadie's Sweet 11."

"What the hell? Sweet 11?" I wondered aloud.

We were ushered through the house to the back yard. I felt sick. The back yard had been transformed into a dream. There was an Olympic-size pool, beautifully wrapped gifts, balloons galore, magicians, pony rides, a DJ, and tables and tables of foods and desserts. Sadie and a few girls from school came running over. Sadie looked like an angel. She was dressed in a beautiful white wedding-style dress that looked like it was made especially for her.

"Sasha! So glad you made it. Are you feeling okay?"

I just stared at her.

"I'm so sorry I didn't wear a purple and green dress like we planned, but I couldn't disappoint my father, who surprised me with this dress this morning. I did wear these ribbons for you, though." She pointed to the purple and green ribbons tied around her head like a headband. "Sasha, thank you for the charm bracelet. I promise I will never take it off."

The DJ announced that it was time to cut the cake. The other girls ushered Sadie away just in time, because I was seconds away from throwing up all over her. All of the guests gathered by the cake.

I moved to where the adults were congregated by the bartender. There were cups left behind on the tables.

I picked up the cups and downed all the "grown folks' candy" I could find. The drinks tasted disgusting and burned the back of my throat. I laid my head down, desperately trying to find a way to stop this rendition of Sadie's perfect life from spinning all around me.

I woke up in a panic. Where was I? I looked around the room, and I saw all the girls from the party. They were all sleeping. My head was killing me. Then, all of the rage started to flood back in. Sadie! This was all her fault. First, she stole the spelling bee from me, then she invited me to her perfect house to show off her perfect life. She was so not my friend. Where was she? I was going to take back my bracelet. She didn't need it. She had everything already.

I got up from the pallet of blankets and went looking for Sadie. I checked all of the sleeping bags next to me, but none of them were her. I counted the sleeping bags and my pallet. Right, there were eight, but now I saw that one bag was empty. I decided to go find Sadie. Come hell or high water, I would get my bracelet back.

I started tiptoeing around her huge perfect house. My stomach started to hurt, my hands started to sweat, my heart beat fast, and I could not stop sneezing. Apparently, I was allergic to perfection. As I approached the long spiral staircase, I started to question my motives. Maybe this wasn't a good idea. If I was caught snooping, surely they would throw me out.

Just as I reached the top of the staircase, I saw a light coming from a bedroom. The door was partially open. I tiptoed closer, drawn like a moth, trying not to sneeze or I'd blow out the flame. I heard voices coming from the room.

"God, grant me the serenity to accept the things I cannot change; courage to change the things I can; and wisdom to know the difference.Living one day at a time; enjoying one moment at a time; accepting hardships as the pathway to peace; taking, as He did, this sinful world as it is, not as I would have it; trusting that He will make all things right if I surrender to His Will; that I may be reasonably happy in this life and supremely happy with Him forever in the next.

Amen," they said in unison.

They got up from their knees and Sadie's mom began to tuck her in. "I told you, honey. There was nothing to worry about. No one noticed your wig, and I will have you back in the morning before the other girls wake up. They won't even know you were gone. This party was everything we planned. Such a gift you are.

The doctors said you wouldn't see eight and here you are, eleven years old."

I watched in awe as Sadie's mom frantically went around the room, making sure everything was in place. Trying to shield her tears. Once satisfied, she smoothed the already smoothed blankets over and over.

"Don't cry, Mom," Sadie said. "This was a beautiful party. I was just a little sad that Sasha wasn't able to be happy with me."

"Sweetie, I don't know what's going on with Sasha, but she does not seem to be okay. Tomorrow, your father and I will take her home and speak to her parents."

"Thanks, Mom. You know that Sasha is my best friend in the whole world, and it hurts me to see her like this."

"I know sweetie. Whatever the problem is, I'm sure we can help."

That's when Sadie's mom did it. She did the thing that allowed me to breathe for the first time since I stepped foot in their damn perfect house. She took Sadie's wig off and put in on a nearby mannequin. I was so shocked and relieved at the same time. Sadie was not perfect.

Suddenly, my hands stopped sweating, my heart beat normally, and the urge to sneeze was gone. I turned and ran as fast as I could back to my pallet. I no longer needed to get the charm bracelet back. I had something so much more powerful. A secret. A secret I could and would use to destroy her perfect world. Just like my life had been destroyed. I would be the drug that came in like a thief in the night to ruin her. I would show her that love loves no one. Including her perfect ass.

The next morning, I woke up pretending to be the old me. I was cheery and sweet when I approached Sadie and another group of girls who were playing with her gifts quietly in a corner of the room.

Sadie's parents arranged for a catered breakfast on the veranda before we went home. The food was exquisite. I was able to stow away a few apples and oranges for me and Sarah for later. All the while, I kept my eye on Sadie. I noticed for the first time that her eyebrows looked drawn on, and that she always wore a headband that I thought was for fashion but I now knew was to keep the wig in place.

Sadie's mom pulled me to the side after breakfast and asked if everything was okay at home. I lied and said that all was well. I just missed my father so badly; he was away on business. I asked her to please forgive my behavior from the night before. I continued, saying that this was just the longest time I had spent away from Dad and it hurt something awful. Sadie's mom said she understood. She said she had planned on talking to my parents, but given the situation, she was sure that everything would return to normal once my father returned. If only she knew.

Jennifer's parents arrived at noon to take us home.

Home, home, home. What an atrocity. The house had an overwhelming smell of smoke from the kitchen fire. Plates of food laid on the coffee table. Pillows were thrown all around the room, the T.V was blaring infomercials. Mom was still laying in the same spot on the couch as the day before. Sarah was in the corner with a handful of dry cat food, trying to put it into Snow's mouth. As I got closer, I could see that Snow had a mouth full of uneaten cat food. Her eyes were closed, and she was not moving.

Sarah kept repeating, "Eat, Snow. Eat, Snow."

That was the final straw. The room went dark as I picked up the dead cat and shoved it in my mother's face.

"Wake up!" I shouted. "We will not live like this anymore. Get up, get up right now and go take a shower.

Mother! Do you hear me? Wake up and fix our lives! Dad may not ever come back, but we can't continue to live like this. We need you, Mom! Get up!" I screamed. "Get up right now!"

I shook Mom with all the strength I could muster. "Mom, wake up and see that our lives are falling apart!" My voice started to crack. "Please Mom! Wake up!"

Mom, as if in a dream, started to come to. She stared at me with her huge brown eyes, and it was like she could see me for the first time in a long time. Mom slowly sat up and looked around the room. She finally said, "Sasha, take that dead cat outside. Whew! I need a shower. You take the cat outside and bury it. I'm going to go take a shower, and when I come down we are going to figure out what is that burning smell."

I looked at her in disbelief. Could it be that Mom was back from wherever she had gone in her mind? I didn't want to give her the opportunity to go back, so I put Snow down and tried to help her off the couch, noticing, for the first time, the bulge in her stomach.

Wow, she really is pregnant, I thought.

She jokingly pushed me off of her, saying, "I got this, Sasha."

I watched her disappear up the staircase before I dared to move. When I heard the water from the shower start, I picked up Sarah and Snow and carried them out back. I explained to Sarah that Snow went to heaven to play with the other cats. I seriously doubted she understood anything that I said, because all she kept saying was "Eat, Snow."

I found a small, rusty shovel in the shed and dug a shallow grave. A thought came to mind as I filled the grave of how lucky Snow was. She was free from this craziness. The thought quickly vanished when I heard Mom come humming her favorite tune from the Spinners, "Could it Be I'm Falling in Love?" I wondered if it could be that Mom was truly back.

"Sasha!" she yelled. "What the hell happened to my kitchen?"

Oh, yeah. Mom was back.

Over the next few weeks, Mom began to slowly piece back what had become of our lives as I went to school to rapidly destroy Sadie's. As I look back on my actions, they weren't something I actually had control over. Just the sight of Sadie made me sick. Monday morning, she came to school so happy. Dressed headband to toe in brand-new clothes. She walked around school like life was all good, not a care in the world.

Well, I was going to show her. Effective immediately, Sadie was going to get a glimpse of how hellish life could be. She was going to have an unveiling party today, and she didn't even know it.

I had to be strategic. Pick a time of day where I could get the largest amount of students to see her and her bald head. Maybe at recess. I could challenge her to a cartwheel contest and maybe it would fall off then. *No,* I thought. Recently, I couldn't convince her to play kickball anymore. She was either tired or had some other lame excuse as to why she couldn't play. Most recently, she told me that God told her that she wasn't supposed to be a tomboy anymore. She said she had to start wearing skirts and dresses to school every day. I tried to convince her otherwise, but that was when we were friends. Before she stole the spelling bee from me and before she invited me to her perfect house with her perfect family. If recess would not work, I would have to do it at lunch.

"Sasha, Sasha, over here," I heard Sadie say at lunch. I had done my best to avoid her all day. Now here she was calling me like we were best friends and she hadn't done anything wrong. Ooooh, I was going to show her.

I slowly walked over in her direction and carried a tray of school lunch. As I got closer to her, envy and jealousy took over even more. She was sitting at a picnic-style lunch table with two other girls from the party. They were talking loudly, reminiscing on the "fabulous Sweet 11." I put one foot over the bench and pretended to lose my balance. I threw my lunch tray to the ground and grabbed on to Sadie's wig to regain control. I intentionally pulled Sadie's wig off before I landed on the floor. A hush fell over the cafeteria.

"Oh my God, Sadie, your hair just came off. Oh my God, is this a wig? Were you wearing a wig all this time?" I shrilled.

In the loudest voice I could find, I shouted again, "Look everyone, Sadie wears wigs and she is bald."

Sadie just sat there with a blank look on her face. I watched in ecstasy as the blood left her rosy cheeks.

I continued, "Why didn't you tell me? We were friends who shared everything. Don't you think I would have wanted to know that my best friend was bald-headed?"

Sadie sat there trying to look like she wasn't there. I stopped to look around the cafeteria, expecting to see the other kids laughing and pointing, but what I saw only added even more fuel to the fire. Everyone was staring at me like I had gone mad. The girls at the table with Sadie moved closer to her and put their arms around her. Sadie put her head down on the table and I saw her shoulders moving.

"Crying? Are you crying? I am the one who should be crying." I threw the long, curly blond wig into what remained of my lunch and stomped on it. "I hate you, Sadie," I yelled over and over until the lunch aide came and escorted me to the principal's office.

The lunch aide left me alone in the principal's office and said something under her breath as she left. I couldn't see or hear anything. The room was red with hate. For the first time in a long time, I cried. I cried for me, for Dad, for Mom, for Sarah, for Sadie, for Snow, for the monster I had become who could do what I had just done to my friend.

I cried. I cried because even though Mom seemed back to her normal self, it was three months late and $10,000 short. She explained to me last night that we were three months behind on the mortgage. She said that the furniture and the cars would be repossessed and we would only pack a few personal belongings to bring with us to Grandmother's house before the sheriff came and threw everything else on the street.

I cried. I cried because Mom told me she needed me to be mature through all of this. She said the baby would be here in just a few short months and she was going to need my help. She needed me to be strong and not to worry about the things we were going to lose. I asked her about school and my friends. Mom said it was best for me to forget about all of that. According to the last letter on the door, we only had a few more days left before we had to vacate the premises. I cried.

After a long time passed, the principal finally came into her office. She sat quietly across from me for a long while. "Sasha," she finally managed. "Sadie told us that none of this is your fault. She says it was just an accident. The most peculiar thing is that all she seems to care about is how you are feeling. Shame, really. Your behavior. We have gotten wind of your little drunken stunt at Sadie's slumber party. That behavior will not be tolerated at this school. Neither will outbursts like you just performed in the cafeteria. Consider this your final warning. Leave from my sight right now."

With that, I slowly left her office. *That little bitch,* I thought. Still managing to come out on top. Having the staff and the other kids feel sorry for her like she was the victim. The hell with that. I was going to ruin Sadie and this perfect life of hers before the sheriff even had a chance to throw us on the street.

Over the next few days the monster inside of me became a lot more creative. Not only had I come up with a song to sing every time I saw Sadie, but I was even able to convince a few loners to join me. You remember Miss Mary Mack? Well we had,

Miss Sadie bald, bald, bald
all dressed in baldness, baldness, baldness
with drawn-in eyebrows, eyebrows, eyebrows
all over her face, face, face
she asked the doctor, doctor, doctor
for some hair, hair, hair
to go to school, school, school
that wouldn't come off, off, off
every time she coughed, coughed, coughed

The loners and I would clap our hands and pat our laps like those were the original words to the song. Singing at lunch and recess where Sadie was sure to hear the words. For the life of me, I couldn't figure out why she still wore that damn charm bracelet. Whenever I made eye contact with her, she looked at me with such a patient and kind eye. Oh, dear God, I hated that girl.

The more compassion Sadie showed me, the angrier I became. I started throwing things at her. I tripped her coming up and down the halls. I taunted her: "Sadie wets the bed at night, Sadie's house is covered in fleas, Sadie can't play kickball anymore because she has a vagina." Anything and everything I could think of to hurt her, I tried, all to no avail. Sadie remained stoic, unmoved, courageous. There were times that I would look at her and just want to throw my arms around her neck and beg for forgiveness. I wanted my friend back. I wanted my family back the way we were. I wanted LOVE. These thoughts would evaporate like a mist. Only lasting seconds, and like a flash of lightning, the monster would be back, whispering in my ear, "destroy her."

The perfect opportunity came for me to make that a reality. The school had an art exhibit showcase, and of course, "Your Baldness" was being featured. The art teacher had us draw self portraits. My art looked like Sarah had done it, but Sadie's, of course, came out perfectly. Somehow, she recreated the exact image I had of her at the "sweet 11." An angel. She even tissue-papered a replica of the white dress she wore. Sadie's portrait was going to be the showcase feature. The art club was going to encase it, surround it with lights, and display it last at the exhibit. While they had their plans, "we" had ours.

Since Mom was holding down what was left of the fort, it was easier for me to leave home. The exhibit was at six o'clock, and if I would make my plans come to fruition, I had to get there by five o'clock. So as not to set off any suspicion, I didn't ask for a ride. I caught the county bus to school. I made a quick stop at the art classroom to pick up a few supplies and stored them in my purple bookbag. The art show would be held in the auditorium. I snuck inside, careful not to be seen. I lifted the curtain and went backstage.

Bam! There it was. Sadie's masterpiece. The art club had it encased already, and it was on an easel with wheels. I stood there for countless moments just staring at its beauty. How she managed to create such a piece of art, I will never know, but what the audience would see that night would be a true masterpiece done by yours truly.

I pulled off the blond curly yarn that she used for hair. I took a black marker and drew lines on her face, and I splattered red paint all over. I wrote "Sadie is bald" across the top of the portrait. I drew horns on the top of her head. I pulled off the white tissue paper at the bottom that was used for the dress, and I drew a large yellow puddle and wrote, "I like to pee the bed." I put the art back in the encasement and draped it with a black sheet I found lying nearby. With any luck, no one would uncover "the masterpiece" until it was on stage.

Satisfied with what I had created, I covered my head with my hoodie and sat in the back of the audience. I watched parents and children excitedly fill the seats. Just before the lights dimmed, in walked Sadie and her family. Sadie looked sickly. She was leaning on her father for support. Her face was ghostly white, her lips were chapped, and her eyes were only halfway open with dark circles underneath.

Our art teacher, Mrs. Wright, took the stage. She gave a spiel about how excited she was about this year's art work, blah blah blah. I zoned out, not interested in anything but the unveiling.

About an hour went by, and I finally heard Mrs. Wright say, "Our final showcase for the night is a beautiful self portrait done by a very special student, Miss Sadie. I would like to present this myself. After years of being an art teacher, I finally met a student who is a real artist."

She excused herself and went behind the curtain. She wheeled out Sadie's work that was still covered. I felt so giddy inside. "Ladies and gentlemen, I would like to present Sadie!"

She uncovered the artwork, and the crowd went wild. Mrs. Wright started screaming uncontrollably. Sadie's father picked her up and swiftly carried her out of the auditorium. I managed to get a look at her face as they walked past. She had tears in her eyes. Finally, I had done something to get to her. I felt triumphant.

Sadie didn't come to school for a week after the art show. *Wow,* I thought, *I finally ruined her perfect life.* I was proud of myself and ill at the thought of my actions at the same time. Rumors flew around school as to Sadie's whereabouts. Some people said she couldn't handle the torture anymore. Some said she was sick. I added a rumor about her not being able to find her wig.

Toward the end of the week, the kids grew tired of talking about Sadie. They moved on with their normal mundane lives, while I continued to wonder if Sadie was, in fact, sick and shut in. I also worried about when the sheriff would come to throw my family out on the street.

We were already two weeks past the eviction date. Mom said that we would stay until they threw us out. She had me pack as many personal belongings as I could fit into my suitcase. No matter how hard I tried, not even one encyclopedia or trophy would fit.

She said we couldn't afford the storage fees, so everything that had not been repossessed would be on the sidewalk. I had nightmares of my beautiful white bed with its matching dresser and mirror being thrown on the street by zombies with police uniforms on. They would break up my spelling bee trophies, tear my encyclopedias apart page by page, and shatter my mirror. I'd wake up in a cold sweat and stare at my things for the rest of the night, trying to capture the image of them to hold onto forever.

Every day I came home from school, I was terrified it would be my last. Always walking slowly and alone down the hill from the bus stop, afraid to see our furniture on the street and embarrassed the kids would laugh at me. *Whew! Not today*, I thought as I walked into the house. Mom was in the living room with Sarah.

"Come help me with this, Sasha," she yelled when she heard me close the front door.

As I walked into the living room, I saw that she had something covered in a blanket, and she was holding a sledgehammer.

"What's going on?" I asked.

"Now, Sasha, I don't need you to be all dramatic about this, but I had your uncle bring down Miss Piggy from your room. I'm going to have to crack her open so we will have money to hold us over until I'm able to find work after I have the baby."

I froze. Miss Piggy was my three-foot-tall ceramic piggy bank that my father bought for me a few years back. Over the years, I grew to love Miss Piggy. I remember hugging her tight just before bed. As awkward as she first appeared, there was something strangely beautiful about her. Her long blond hair, exaggerated big nose, her long pink dress with her purple gloves that covered her fat hands and arms. Her pearl necklace and white shoes, all about to be shattered by Mom, who had covered her in an old blanket, ready to break her into a million little pieces. She would be shattered. Just like my future.

Dad used to come home with quarters and a few singles. "For my star," he would say. Miss Piggy was for my college fund. He said when she was full, he would buy another and another until all my dreams came true.

"Fine," I heard Mom say. "If you are just going to stand there, I will do it myself."

Mom started swinging the hammer like she had gone mad. The sound of the hammer hitting the ceramic through the blanket shook me to my core. Each blow Mom threw went through me like a lightning jolt. I could see pieces of Miss Piggy's blond hair laying broken among the coins and dollar bills. I thought of Sadie. I thought that wherever she was, sick, avoiding me and my taunts, or looking for her wig, she was in a much better place than me.

The monster inside of me broke my frozen trance. I walked over to Mom, who was in mid-swing, and grabbed the hammer from her hands. I beat Miss Piggy until her head was completely smashed off. I yelled, I screamed, I cried, and I swung until I couldn't swing anymore.

When I was spent and out of breath, Mom said, "Are you done? Now that you have that out of your system, help me clean up the pieces so we can sort through this money." Mom had gone to the bank and gotten the coin wrappers that needed to be filled so the bank would exchange them for cash.

The endless sorting and wrapping seemed to go on for days. Mom worked quietly and quickly stuffing the coin wrappers. She would only stop to make dinner. I would stare at her from time to time, trying to read her mind. To find out how in the hell we had gotten to this point. One night after dinner, Sarah decided to help me and Mom stuff the wrappers. She stuffed the coins in the wrong wrapper and said, "Look Mom, look Sasha."

We mumbled, "Good job Sarah," both of us caught up in our own thoughts. Sarah walked over to where I sat and said "Look Sasha," in a muffled voice.

Without looking at her, I said, "Good job."

She said, "Look, Sasha," again, this time even more strained.

I looked up and saw her pointing to her throat. "Oh, my God, she is choking!" I screamed.

Sarah fell into my lap. "Mom, help me, Sarah is choking on a coin."

Mom sat there for a few seconds, looking like she couldn't move.

"Mom, she's going to die!" I screamed as I watched Sarah's eyes roll back in her head.

Mom snapped out of her trance. She jumped up and grabbed Sarah roughly from my lap. She carried Sarah to the couch. Lunging Sarah head down on her lap, she gave Sarah hard blows to her back.

I jumped up and ran to the coffee table where the phone was. I shakily dialed 911. The operator came on the line.

"911, what's your emergency? Do you need the fire department or an ambulance?"

I looked over at Mom and Sarah.

Mom yelled, "Come out of my baby!" and punched Sarah so hard on the back I thought for sure she was dead. Suddenly, the nickel that was lodged in her throat came flying across the room. Sarah started crying, choking, and coughing. Mom started to cry, too. I hung up the phone. What we needed, 911 could not offer.

The next day at school, I became withdrawn. Walked around like in a dream. Nothing seemed real anymore.

Sadie was back. Looking even more beautiful and radiant than I remembered. Her skin looked slightly tanned. Had she been on vacation? A family vacation to the beach, I imagined. I envisioned her entire family laughing and playing on the beach during the day and fancy dinners at night. I couldn't hate her any more than I did at that moment.

My body felt numb inside. Even when Sadie cornered me in the hall and asked if I could just forgive her for whatever she had done to make me hate her so. Even though I saw a pleading, tired look in her eyes, I just pushed past her without saying a word. How dare she. Still wanting to be my friend after all she had done to me. *I'll just have to show her once and for all that we will never be friends again.*

My opportunity came sooner than I could have imagined. I was called to the principal's office during recess. I sat down in the familiar seat across from Mrs. Brown.

"Sasha," she began, "we have reason to believe that you are the culprit of the destruction of artwork at the art exhibit. Is there anything that you would like to say about that?"

I sat there quietly.

"Sasha, we have evidence that you were at the art show. We have an eyewitness that saw you leaving from backstage. We have countless testimonies from students that say you have been bullying Sadie since the incident in the cafeteria when you pulled her wig off. Which I know was not an accident. If you do not start talking, I am going to expel you immediately."

"I did it," I confessed. "It's true, I destroyed Sadie's artwork, I pulled off her wig in the cafeteria, I pushed her, I made up songs about her, I made other kids not want to play with her. I hate Sadie with all of my heart."

Mrs. Brown sat there, looking shocked. "Is all of this true? You have been bullying my student right under my nose? Why would you do such terrible things? Sadie was your friend. You will stop bullying now if you expect to stay in this school another second."

Mrs. Brown let out a long sigh and put her hand to her forehead.

"Please try to explain why you would do such things to such a beautiful girl."

I started my performance. I began to cry. I put my head down on my forearm on her desk so she couldn't see my eyes. "Sadie deserves everything I did to her and more."

"Whatever do you mean?" Mrs. Brown asked.

I took my time, creating the lie as I went along. "Sadie told me her dad, um, um, touches her private parts at night, and she likes it," I blurted out.

Mrs. Brown was silent. I lifted my head to make sure that she heard me. She was ghostly white, and I repeated what I had said.

"I heard you the first time, Sasha. If this is true, why didn't you tell anyone?"

"I didn't think anyone would believe me. You were so quick to take Sadie's side the day I pulled her wig off. I knew what she told me was disgusting and wrong so I decided to torment her. She is evil and deserves to be punished."

"Did Sadie tell you where her father touches her?"

"Yes," I lied.

Mrs. Brown opened the drawer to her desk and pulled out a naked white baby doll. *Strange,* I thought.

"Point to where she told you he touched her."

I took the doll and laid her down in front of me. I pointed to the doll's vagina and butt, and I said, "She says he likes to kiss her there sometimes, too."

Mrs. Brown looked like she was going to throw up. I guess she had never seen *Nightmare on Elm Street*. She regained her composure and said, "These are very strong accusations. There will be a full investigation. If you are fabricating anything, you had better tell me now."

"It's all true," I said, crossing my heart

Mrs. Brown dismissed me from her office, telling me before I exited not to tell anyone of our conversation until she had a chance to contact Sadie's parents. I left the office feeling like I had finally shown Sadie that I was not playing with her perfect ass. This was going to erupt, and when it did, her family would look up and wonder what the hell happened to their perfect lives. Just like I did. Revenge felt so good.

Surprisingly, days went by and still the sheriff hadn't come. I hadn't seen Sadie in school in the days after my confession. I overheard a teacher tell another teacher that Sadie was desperately sick and in the hospital. *Nice try,* I thought. She was pretending to be ill to avoid an investigation. *She had better stay sick,* I thought.

I wondered which would come first. Sadie to stop pretending to be sick, or the eviction. With any luck, Sadie would be back soon so we could get this show of destroying her life on the road. Maybe the sheriff's department had lost our paperwork and would never come to evict us. Maybe they would go to Sadie's house and take her dad to jail. Then she would know what it's like when your dad doesn't come home. That would be perfect.

I didn't get a chance to have these fantasies for long. All in one day, reality came crashing down on my head.

That school day started out like any other. Of course, Sadie conveniently still hadn't come back to school, and there wasn't any more talk of where she may have been this time.

All questions were answered when Mrs. Brown frantically called me to her office over the loudspeaker. "Sasha, report to my office now!" she screamed. I hurriedly made my way to her office, thinking this was my debut to repeat my lies to the police.

When I walked into her office, she threw an open envelope into my hands and stormed out, leaving me alone. I took a seat and looked into the envelope. Inside were two ribbons. One purple. One green. I nervously opened the folded letter.

Dear Sasha,

Do you remember the day we met? Our first day of kindergarten, I was crying in the corner. You came over and asked me my favorite colors. When I said purple and green, you said you would be my friend and I didn't need to cry anymore. You were the best friend I could have ever asked for. Thank you for coming to get me that day. The doctors say I am not going to make it through the night. I never shared with you, or anyone outside of my family, that for the past four years, I have been battling stage four chronic lymphocytic cancer (that's fancy for I'm very sick). I never told you because I knew you would try to protect me and there was nothing you could have done. Chemotherapy is the medicine that they gave me to fight this disease. It caused all of my hair to fall out. Sorry.

I don't know what has happened to us lately. Whatever it is that you are going through at home that has made you hate me and my family, I am so sorry. I know that it must be terrible to take you away from me.

I need you to know that I forgive you for everything that you have done to me. I have asked my parents to forgive you and they have as well. My dying wish is that you forgive yourself. Don't cry for me. I have accepted death and it's not as scary as it seems. I have peace. My mother has promised to deliver this letter to you once I am gone.

Thank you for being my friend. Love often, laugh often, play and spell often.

P.S. I will never take off the bracelet you gave me.

Your friend forever,
Sadie

I slid to the floor and crawled under Mrs. Brown's desk. I tried to process what I had just read. No way Sadie was dead. I hugged the letter to my legs for dear life. Trying desperately and unsuccessfully to breathe life back into my friend through her words.

I stayed under that desk until the bell for dismissal rang. Somehow, I boarded the school bus home. When I exited the bus, my legs wouldn't move. I stayed there, stuck, for a very long time. At some point, Mom drove up the hill. She spotted me at the bus stop.

"Sasha, there you are! Get your ass in the car. The sheriff came today. That's it, we are leaving."

That was it. No chance to say goodbye to anything or anyone. I'd never see my home again. My bedroom, my spelling bee trophies, my encyclopedias that were too big to fit in the suitcase. Everything was gone in a blink of an eye. Here I was sitting next to Mom in her Cadillac that she said they would have to find if they wanted to repossess, with Sarah in her car seat in the back, headed on the eight-hour drive to Grandmother's house.

I pulled the ribbons Sadie sent from my pocket, and I replayed the letter over and over in my head. It hit me like a ton of bricks. My best friend was dying all along, and instead of loving her, I tormented her. I started screaming. I screamed and screamed until I eventually passed out.

PART 2

"Daddy, Daddy," I yelled as I ran into his arms. His Cool Water cologne brought back all kinds of nostalgia. Dad picked me up and threw me high up in the air. I landed in his arms, and he hugged me tight. He kissed me with a big wet kiss on the cheek.

"Sasha, I've missed you, girl. Let's ride, just me and you like old times."

We walked, hand in hand, outside, where there was a brand new convertible, a candy apple green Cadillac, waiting for us. We rode into the sunset, listening to music, laughing, and reminiscing. I was intoxicated with love, feeling light and worry-free. We followed the beacon of the northern star. The wind tried mercilessly to let loose my captive braids while the shadows of the sun warmed my skin.

As the pavement was lost for miles behind us, I looked ahead and saw a bright future for our family. "Dad," I said, "Where have you been? Let's go back and get Mom and Sarah. Mom will forgive you for everything. Just one look at you, and she will forgive you, like always."

Dad turned to me with a look of sadness and hopelessness. He popped the tape out of the tape deck. "Sasha," he started quietly, "I cannot do that right now. I have some things I need to work out on my own. Life is not good for me right now. I have many demons inside that I am battling."

"What?" I almost whispered. "You have demons inside? Well, we have demons outside, all around us. Do you know what life has been like for us since you left? Do you have any idea?"

Dad drove the car and stared straight ahead. He pushed the tape back into the tape deck. The Spinners came on loud over the new sound system. *"It Takes A Fool..."*

I woke up in a cold sweat. Oh, no, I had done it again. It wasn't sweat. I had wet the bed again. I looked over to Sarah sleeping next to me on the twin bed. Yep, she was wet, too. I was running out of excuses as to why she kept waking up wet. Just a couple of feet away, Mom slept on the other twin bed in the motel room.

We had been here for a week. After we had been driving south for an awful long time, Mom explained that she had a change of plans. We were not going to Grandmother's house. She said that she had talked to

Dad, and he was living in Florida. She said Florida was a beautiful place. She said the fruit grew on trees, the beaches were the bluest, the grass was the greenest you had ever seen, and the sun kissed your skin. Mom talked the entire way. More to herself than to me and Sarah. We stopped frequently, so the trip was forever long. Not that it mattered. We were all caught up in our own thoughts. Mourning the lives we left behind.

While Miami, Florida, was the most beautiful place I had ever seen, this motel was by far the worst. Mom said we had to stay somewhere affordable until Dad was able to find us a house. I was convinced this place was affordable because they must have paid us to stay here. This hideous motel with its yellow chipped paint, dirty brown, stained carpet, the smell of mold, the empty rusty pool and, worst of all, the flying cockroaches that were everywhere. If Sarah was more afraid of them than me, you wouldn't have known it, because whenever we saw one, we both would take off running and screaming to Mom. Mom would just shoo us away and tell us to get used to them.

This trip took a lot out of Mom. She looked tired and worried. She constantly went back and forth to the front desk calling Dad. I knew when she spoke with him and when she had not. She either came back to the room with a look of doom or pure relief.

She started talking out loud again. It seemed she was trying to convince herself that everything would be okay. She would say, "He will find a real nice house real soon and he will come to get us. I'll register Sasha in her new school, I'll have this baby and lose this weight. We will buy better furniture than what we had. I'll buy a brand-new Cadillac, we will make new friends. Everything is going to be just fine."

Dad came a few days later. He had lost a lot of weight. His eyes were yellow and wild, his clothes were shabby, and he smelled of beer, but he came. Mom and Sarah were so happy to see him, so I pretended to be. We packed up our few belongings in Mom's car, and we drove to the "fancy new house" Dad raved about. I must admit, I started to get excited when I heard about the large, four-bedroom, single-family house. The massive back yard with a screened-in porch. The lake, he excitedly described, was huge enough to go fishing in. Mom looked at my dad like he had saved the day.

I had so many questions and felt so many emotions. Who, what, where, when, and most importantly, why? It was very hard for me to understand, but I told myself that Mom must know what she was doing.

I let my guard down when he asked if we wanted to stop by the beach before we drove home. Sarah and I screamed "Yes!" from the backseat.

We rode for another hour before we reached the beach. It was truly breathtaking. The way the sun touched the ocean, the sound of the waves hitting the land. The exotic birds that flew overhead. The brown sugar sand that met the beautiful translucent blue water. I could have sworn I heard voices in the whirling wind calling out to me. Strong voices telling me I was not alone and not to be afraid. The beach felt like home, a new home. A home that the sheriff couldn't come and throw me out of. A peace, a calm, a sense of belonging. The ocean, a place I would forever call home and a place I never wanted to leave.

Sarah and I walked out into the ocean with our T-shirts and shorts on. We splashed water on each other and built sand castles using discarded trash as our shovels and buckets because we had not been prepared for this impromptu stop.

After hours of frolicking, we reluctantly climbed back into Mom's car, wet and sandy, wishing we had at least one towel. Sand was in our hair, eyes, ears, and everywhere else you could imagine. It was not a good feeling. Dad quieted our complaints by telling us the new house was just a few more minutes away.

As we approached the house, Dad yelled, "This is it!"

"Wow," we all said at the same time. The house was spectacular.

"Can we really afford this?" Mom asked.

"Yes, honey, I got a great deal on it. I told you the rent down here is cheap anyway, but I got an even better deal 'cause the house needs some work."

Work? I wondered, because this house looked picture-perfect.

As soon as the car stopped in the two-car driveway, we all jumped out, super excited to see the inside. Dad made a production about finding the key.

"Come on, Dad," I whined.

He produced the key and unlocked the door.

"Wow," we all said again. What a beautiful tiled foyer. We all walked in, still sandy from the beach, and Sarah and I started to run around. Opening doors and admiring the space. The first floor was amazing. It had a massive eat-in kitchen, separate dining room, oversized living room, and the lake in the back yard looked adventurous.

"Mom," I said, "Dad was right, this house is fancy."

I opened another door on the first floor. "This must be the guest bedroom," I assumed. It was a fairly large bedroom with a full bathroom. I grabbed Sarah by the hand. "Let's go pick out our new room," I said heading for the staircase.

Dad appeared abruptly from the kitchen. "No!" he yelled. "That's what I have been trying to tell you guys all along. The entire top level of the house is infested with fleas. No one will ever go up there until I say it is okay. Do you all hear me?"

We all nodded our heads in affirmation. Mom started to flick sand from her hair and asked, "Is there anything else we need to know?"

"Yeah, the water and the electric won't be on until next week," Dad said as he grabbed Mom's keys from the countertop and walked out the front door.

Three months passed. Instead of the nightmare ending, it actually got worse. The electricity did eventually come on. The water, not so much. When my dad was around, he would run a water hose from the neighbor's house once they left for work. He would flush the toilet and fill jugs of water. We all took occupancy in the one bedroom on the first floor. There was a bed that Mom and Dad slept in, and Sarah and I slept on pallets on the floor. Mom's stomach continued to swell, and for fun we thought of baby names. Sarah wanted to name the baby Curly Sue after her favorite movie. Mom promised that if the baby had curly hair, she would name her Suzanne and we would call her Curly Sue.

We watched hours on end of our favorite TV shows and movies. *Curly Sue, The Last Unicorn, ThunderCats, Home Alone, Labyrinth, The NeverEnding Story, Days Of Our Lives, As The World Turns*. Sadly, nothing could have prepared me for what was in store.

June 19th. June 19th. Juneteenth. I had a special connection with my grandfather. I was born on his birthday. Grandfather shared things with me that were important to him. Our ancestors were very important to Grandfather. He would always say, "You can't know where you are going until you know where you've been." He told me to make sure I listened to his words, because what he was telling me I'd never find in the encyclopedias I liked to read. June 19th is the day "a large percentage of our ancestors found out they were free from slavery. Now, President Lincoln had signed the emancipation proclamation in 1863, but, the tale goes, they deliberately kept the news from slaves to maintain the labor force. You being the first born grandchild, born on my birthday and the day a lot of our ancestors found out they were free, is a sign from God. Juneteenth is a day of celebration. A day to be celebrated. The day we celebrate you and our ancestors who came before us."

I laid there thinking about my ancestors. How they stayed enslaved two years longer because they just didn't get the news that they were free. I laid there hoping that Mom and Dad just didn't get the news that today was June 19th. I laid there trying, unsuccessfully, not to move, think, or breathe. If I stopped breathing, that would conclude this feeling of absolute disappointment. That would end the realization that an entire day had gone by and no one had uttered the words "happy" or "birthday." The disappointment resonated through my soul. It was like a drug that filled and flowed through my veins. Without it, I would have had nothing.

I spent the entire day peeping out the windows, waiting for my dad to show up with even the slightest sign of celebration. He never came. I laid there feeling broken. Broken like my ancestors must have felt. Broken like Mom, who I saw crying when she thought I wasn't looking. Broken like Dad, who would constantly complain that he was broke and that was the reason the lights were off again. Broken were my dreams for a bright future. Broken like Miss Piggy. Broken and empty inside. Broken were the images and memories of the home we left behind. Broken was my half of the charm bracelet that originally represented a bond with a friend but now only reminded me of the bond I broke. Broken was the hope for a birthday cake, one balloon, one green or purple streamer, one look of love from Mom and Dad, one kiss, one hug, one gift, one friend, one happy birthday song. It was all broken. Never to be redeemed. My eleventh birthday. Broken.

Dad did come home a few days later. He was in an exceptionally good mood. Sadly, his mood did not match his hygiene. He had us all gather in the kitchen and wait, because he had a surprise for us. He quickly walked out the front door. I desperately tried not to get excited. Given Dad's appearance and the funk that lingered in the air, the only surprise he could have given us was a bath. But despite myself, I did get excited. Hoping that Dad did remember my birthday.

Dad came into the kitchen carrying a very small fish tank. Inside was a large white bunny rabbit. He sat the tank down on the kitchen floor. We hesitantly inched closer. Dad spoke too fast about how he caught the rabbit because he just knew that Sarah would want to have it.

"Sarah would want to have it?" I asked, trying to hold back my tears.

Not noticing my eyes turning red or the crack in my voice, Dad said, "Yeah, the rabbit is not for you. It's for Sarah."

Sarah walked up to the fish tank and said, "Hello, Skippy."

I ran from the house. I ran until I realized that love was not chasing me.

That night, while everyone was asleep, I snuck into the kitchen. I saw Skippy in the corner in the fish tank, a piece of plywood partially covering the top so he couldn't hop out. I bent down next to the tank. I looked deep into Skippy's red eyes, and I saw what had become of our lives.

I thought back to good times. When Mom and Dad bragged to their friends about how good life was. The elaborate parties, the fancy meals, the music, the cars, the clothes, the spas. All gone.

Before I knew what was happening, I completely covered the fish tank with the plywood. There was no way Dad brought home a rabbit for my little sister. It wasn't her birthday. It was mine. I deserved the rabbit. I deserved to be thought of on the day that was meant for celebration. Not Sarah.

After a long while, Skippy started to panic. I saw his leg start to twitch. He was losing oxygen. I thought back to June 19th. The night I hoped I could lose oxygen. The night I tried to stop the disappointment with suffocation. Death. A dark tunnel Skippy couldn't realize was so much better than this hellhole.

"Goodbye, Skip," I whispered. "I'll tell Sarah you said goodbye."

The following morning, I was the first one awake. I was anxious to see the look of death on Skippy's face, and more importantly, the look of sadness on Sarah's.

"Sarah, wake up. Let's go play with Skippy."

Sarah sat up and wiped the sleep from her eyes. Just the sound of Skippy's name was enough to have her up and running toward the kitchen.

Screams filled the house. Mom and Dad jumped out of bed and ran toward the kitchen.

I laughed and watched everyone's reaction from the bedroom. Sarah had fallen to the floor. She cried and screamed, "Skippy's dead," over and over.

Dad picked Sarah up and tried to console her. Mom rubbed her back. Dad promised he would chase another rabbit down, one better than Skippy.

I walked into the kitchen and tried to act concerned. "What is going on? What happened to Skippy?"

Mom and Dad shrugged. Dad said he was sure he hadn't left the lid on too tight.

"Maybe the rabbit jumped and accidentally covered the lid," I offered.

"Maybe," Mom and Dad said in unison.

Or maybe, I thought, *revenge still feels so good.*

School didn't start for another couple of weeks. Mom was able to convince my old school that she had homeschooled me and I was ready for the sixth grade. It was mostly true. I had learned a lot in home economics.

The upstairs of the house would remain off limits the entire duration of our stay. Curiosity got the best of me one day, so I went up while Mom napped. I slowly walked up the stairs, not knowing what to expect. I actually hadn't ever seen a flea. I knew they lived on cats and dogs, but I hadn't ever seen one.

The upstairs took my breath away. There was a long hall of plush carpet, shimmering white walls, and so much space. All the bedroom doors were closed, so I cautiously opened each one. The rooms were huge. Each with large windows and closets. I imagined my furniture from my old bedroom in here, and I suddenly felt nauseous.

I backed out of one room and walked farther down the hall. The master bedroom was stupendous. Even with every piece of Mom's furniture from the townhouse, this room would have still looked empty. It was massive, with skylights and a balcony.

"Why was Dad keeping all of this from us? I don't see any fleas."

I walked into the master bath, amazed by the double sinks, jacuzzi tub, and separate shower. I couldn't help but climb into the empty tub. I laid my head back on the cool porcelain and tried to remember the feeling of a warm bath.

I suddenly felt something jumping on me. I opened my eyes and looked down at my body. I was covered in fleas. I jumped out of the tub and started to scream, "Fleas, fleas, get them off of me!"

I ran downstairs and out the back door. I ran straight into the lake without any hesitation. I completely submerged my body and stayed underwater until I was convinced each flea had drowned.

I laid back in the water and began to float. I tried to keep my mind on how this was as close to a warm bath that I had had in months.

Over the next few weeks, Mom was able to do less and less. Her hands and feet swelled, and it hurt her to move. The baby was coming any day. I waited on her hand and foot.

There was a convenience store not too far from the house. Mom gave me a ten-dollar bill and told me to bring back bread, milk, and cereal so Sarah and I would have food to hold us over until she came back from having the baby. She reminded me over and over to bring back her change.

I always enjoyed the walk to the store. I picked oranges from the trees along the way. They tasted so sweet, and they helped keep me cool from the hot Florida sun. The worst part of the walk was the dual highway I has to cross. I was instructed to cross at the crosswalk, but it was a ten-minute walk out of the direction of the store. I decided to take my chances. I waited for the perfect opportunity to cross. No cars were coming either way, and I ran. Whew, I made it.

Inside the Piggly Wiggly (what a name for a store), I picked out the items on the list and a grape funpak. *A service charge*, I thought. The woman behind the counter rung up my order like I was inconveniencing her. She had overwhelmingly bad pimply, oily, dark skin.

She threw my groceries into two bags and said in an accent that I could barely understand, "Your total is $9.23."

I asked, "$9.23?"

She popped her gum and rolled her eyes. "What you said."

I handed her the ten dollars. She threw the seventy-seven cents into my hand. I took the bags in my other hand and rushed out of the store.

As I approached the highway this time, I got a nervous feeling in my stomach. Maybe I should walk to the crosswalk. "No, these bags are heavy," I said aloud.

I looked to the left, and there weren't any cars coming. Safe that way. I looked to the right, and there was a car passing me. I started to walk. This was definitely the better way.

A car came flying behind me, beeping its horn, catching me off guard. I stumbled on something in the road and dropped the money in the street. All I could see was all the hard work me and Mom put into wrapping the coins. I saw Sarah choking on a coin, and I absentmindedly crouched down and picked up the money.

Something hit my side with a force I cannot describe. I smelled burned rubber, and I felt myself fly into the air. I came falling down headfirst into the yellow curb. Everything went black.

The familiar rays of the sun blinded me in my sleep. I opened my eyes, and I was surrounded by darkness. I started squirming. Everything hurt. My head felt like fireworks were going off.

"Be still, Sasha," I heard an unfamiliar voice say. "Do you know where you are?"

I thought I said, "No," but I didn't hear my voice. Tears stung my eyes.

The person I could not see said, "Don't cry, Sasha. You are okay. You are in the hospital. You have been hit by a car and sustained a gash to your forehead. The bandages must stay in place for another day or so. There is nothing wrong with your vision. But your eyes must stay covered for now."

I started to lick my lips, and my mouth was parched. Had I been chewing on gravel, too? Talking was not an option, and I laid there thinking about what the woman had said and trying to remember if what she said was the truth.

For the life of me, I couldn't remember. While I lay there soaked in darkness, all I could vividly see was Sadie's beautiful face. She was angelic. She was smiling in some images, laughing in others, but I knew she was happy, and more importantly, she was still my friend.

"Sadie! I called out to her. "There is so much I want to say to you, so much to explain."

She quieted me with a, "Shhh." "There is nothing that you need to say, Sasha. You have been forgiven. I am in a better place because now I can watch over you. I have so much I need to say to you, so just listen before the doctor comes back."

I nodded.

"You are going to never look the same as you did before this car accident. Sasha, there is a darkness that is trying to take over you. As long as you continue to think negatively of your situation, you will attract negativity. Until you start to fight back, and change the way you think and behave, you will not be saved."

"Saved?" I wondered.

"Yes, Sasha, saved by God. Just listen, there are things that are going to happen to you that are beyond your control, but you can control how you react. The things that will happen to you are not your fault, and especially not your sister's fault. Fight the darkness, Sasha. It will be hard, but I know you can do it. Say it with me. Fight the darkness, fight the darkness."

A gentle hand shook me awake. "Sasha, wake up, you are talking in your sleep."

I opened my eyes, and for the first time I was able to see. I looked around the room. An old white man in a doctor's coat told me his name. He explained to me everything the woman had said. He also explained that while I was sleeping, he had removed my bandages. He wanted to know if I preferred to wait until my mother returned to see the damage.

Damage? I heard Sadie's voice say again, "You are never going to look the same." I closed my eyes and tried to shut out the world.

I woke up to the sound of a baby crying. Mom was holding my hand. She was wearing a hospital gown like mine. Sarah was in a chair watching "Tom and Jerry," and there was a bassinet in the corner filled, I assumed, with the baby I heard. Mom had tears in her eyes.

"Hi, Mom," I said groggily. "I think I lost your change."

"Oh, Sasha," she said. "No one is worried about that change. You scared me to death. How do you feel?"

"I'm fine, Mom," I lied. "Is that the baby over there?"

"Yes," she said, looking away. "Sasha, have you seen your face?"

"Not yet," I said dismissively. "Can I see the baby? What did you name her?"

Mom waved me off, saying, "There is plenty of time for that." She looked worried and a bit scared.

"What's wrong?" I asked.

"Sasha, the doctor says you need to see your face so you can start to deal with how you look now."

Immediately, I was so afraid to ever look into a mirror again. Between Sadie's message, the doctor's reference to "damage," and the panicked look in Mom's eyes, no thanks.

The baby started to cry louder. "Mom," I said, "how about we do it at the same time? Bring the mirror and the baby."

Mom hesitantly agreed. She walked over to the bassinet and lovingly lifted the baby into her arms. She walked to my hospital bed and picked up the hand-held mirror. She handed me the mirror first. I put it on the bed, then she placed the baby in my arms. Sarah crawled up into the bed with us, too. The baby was wrapped up in blanket, so I couldn't see her face. I decided to look at my face first.

I lifted the mirror and turned it over. The reflection staring at me so closely resembled the destruction I did to Sadie's artwork that I thought I was dreaming. There was a large stitched-up gash in the center of my forehead, scabs that had slightly started to heal, and dried patches of blood. I put the mirror down, convinced that was not me. Since it wasn't me, but Sadie getting back at me for destroying her art, no reaction was necessary.

I looked down at the wrapped baby, and I was so excited to meet her. Sarah inched closer on the bed, keeping her eyes on the baby and off of my face. "Curly Sue," Sarah said as I unwrapped the tiny baby. The first thing I noticed was this head full of curly, black, shiny hair. Her skin was the color of a prized brown sweet potato. Her eyes were beautifully round, and her cheeks were soft and fat. She was perfect.

Tears came to my eyes. Mom wiped my tears with a tissue. "Sasha, you are going to be okay," Mom said over and over. Again, I felt like she was trying to convince herself more than me.

The doctor released us all the following day. Mom and baby were fine. Doctor sent me home with a bottle of painkillers and a speech about looking both ways before crossing the street. Dad was waiting for us in a broken-down car I didn't recognize. I didn't even bother to ask where Mom's car was, and neither did she. When we got home, Mom and Dad scrambled around trying to get us settled into the one bedroom we all still shared.

There was now a bassinet for the baby, but Sarah and I still slept on the floor. Dad, who appeared and disappeared so often that no one even asked where he had been, prepared his signature meal that night. Fried chicken and sliced fried potatoes. It tasted like home. We ate on the blanket in the dining room, and Mom and Dad tried to prepare me for my first day of school. I half-listened while I tried to erase the memories from my past and prepare to make new ones.

First day of school was unlike any other first day. No new clothes, backpack, shoes, new hair style, spa day, nothing. I showered, thankful for at least one luxury, and dressed in a plain white T-shirt and some cutoff jeans. Mom handed me a bag lunch and told me to follow the other kids to the bus stop.

As I boarded the bus, I tried unsuccessfully to find a friendly face. I stared at the floor of the bus until we arrived at the school. Everything was so unfamiliar and hideously beautiful. The large palm trees shading the dilapidated building. The florescent orange and yellows painted on cracked rusted walls. The greenest grass growing sporadically in small patches of hard cracked dirt. The woman at the front desk who had the whitest teeth and the darkest skin walked me to my class.

She spoke to the teacher. "Mrs. April, this is your new student. Her name is Sasha, and she is not from around here."

Her accent was so thick I had to read her lips to understand. Thankfully, she talked super slow. The teacher, whose accent was the same and who also talked like she was reading a book to a baby, said, "Hello, Sasha, tell the class your name and where you are from."

I looked at her in astonished disbelief. Did Mom tell her I lost all common sense in the accident? Why were they all talking like this? Then I remembered the girl's accent from the Piggly Wiggly. Maybe this was how everyone spoke in Florida.

I stepped into the center of the classroom. I looked around at the students who were all black, which was disturbing enough, but they also looked malnourished, ashy, and nappy.

I started to say, "My name is Sasha. I am from--" when all the children started to laugh.

"What's wrong with her voice?" a loud-mouthed boy from the back of the room shouted.

Then another boy yelled, "Man, fuck her voice, what the hell happened to her face?"

A girl up front said slowly, "She sounds like a white girl, but she looks like Harriet Tubman with that gash on her forehead."

I ran from the classroom. I ran down the dimly lit halls, searching for a place to hide in the open.

The days I did go to school, I came home and took my frustrations out on Sarah. Not sure if it was the constant teasing, name calling, evil looks, the hitting, the feeling of being left out, or just plain old not being able to fit in at school that pushed me over the edge with Sarah. Not sure when the transition came of me feeling like I had to protect my sister to when she became the enemy. Whatever or whenever it was, the monster inside me had me doing things to my middle sister that were beyond evil. The bed, or should I say pallet, wetting intensified. I no longer made up excuses as to why the blankets and her pajamas were wet.

One night Sarah, accidently, I'm sure, peed on my blanket. When I woke up the following morning and saw her next to me laying in a wet spot, I lost it.

"Bedwetter!" I teased. "How would you like it if I peed on your blankets?"

I moved to where Sarah's blankets were and laid down. I pulled down my pajama bottoms and underwear and intentionally peed all over her blankets.

Sarah started to wail. Mom woke and looked down at us from the bed. Sarah tried to tell her what I had done. Mom told Sarah to go back to sleep as she rolled back over. The darkness was winning again.

Months passed. The seasons didn't change, but our lives did. I didn't go to school. I listened at night on the pallet next to Mom and Dad's bed. I listened to the sound of them either rubbing private parts or arguing. Not sure which was more entertaining. I closed my eyes and imagined them doing the things me and the boys from my closet did. They sure did make the same noises.

Mom and Dad "being nasty" didn't last as long as their arguments. They weren't the loud yelling and screaming kind of arguments anymore. It was more pleading and begging for Dad to try harder.

One night as I lay there, waiting to hear what the night would bring, I heard Mom tell Dad some disturbing news. "I think I'm pregnant again," she said.

Dad said nothing.

She let out a sigh and said, "I think there is something wrong with Curly Sue."

Dad asked, "What?" in a nonchalant voice.

"Not sure, I just feel like something is wrong."

"Nothing is wrong with that baby. You are just trying to find something wrong with everything and everybody, just like you keep telling me I have a drug problem. There is nothing wrong with me, and there is nothing wrong with that baby."

Dad got up and put his pants back on.

"Where are you going?" Mom asked, her voice hurt.

"Somewhere to think. I can't think in here with you."

One day, a woman came to the door, asking to speak with Mom. I looked over my shoulder at the sheer chaos behind me. This woman, with her nice dress, hair, and shoes should not step foot in this house. I started to say no when Mom called my name and asked who was at the door.

The woman walked past me and let herself in. She stopped in the middle of the foyer and started to cover her nose. I looked around at what could have been a beautiful house that was still shockingly empty of furnishings. Bare walls and too many people crammed in one floor of living space. There were dirty dishes in the sink, dirty clothes thrown all over the floor, dirty diapers laid around, and crayon marks on the walls. Chaos.

Mom appeared from the back room carrying Curly Sue in one arm with a red scarf tied around her head. "Can I help you?" Mom asked the woman.

"No, you cannot. But I can help you. My name is not important. I am here to share the word of the Lord and find out if you have a church home."

Mom looked annoyed. "Look, lady, as you can see, I don't have time for that."

The woman interjected, "Actually ma'am, you will make time for God or He will make you make time for Him."

Mom looked confused, and the woman continued. "Ma'am, are you a child of God? Have you accepted Him into your heart? Do you know Him for yourself?"

Mom began to cry. The woman told Mom that she could feel that Mom knew who God was.

"God led me here to your house today to lead you back to the Word."

Mom looked like she would fall, so I went to take Curly Sue before she did. Mom asked me to take the girls into the bedroom we all shared. I turned the TV on low so I could still hear the conversation and cracked the door so I could see.

"Ma'am, God is a forgiving God. As long as you confess with your mouth, "Jesus is Lord," and believe with your heart that God raised Him from the dead, you will be saved."

Mom just cried. The woman encouraged Mom to repeat a prayer after her. I suddenly remembered Sadie telling me in the hospital that I could be saved, so I closed my eyes and repeated the prayer with Mom. The woman said "Amen," after the prayer. She then said that Mom's name was now written in the book of life.

I imagined God writing my name into the large book of life too, and I felt the darkness start to fade.

The woman got up from where she was sitting on the floor and gave Mom a business card. "This is the name of the church where I belong. Please come by for Bible study on Wednesday and church service on Sunday. Bring the children. They will love it."

Mom walked the woman to the door, not saying anything. The woman seemed content. Mom closed the door behind the woman. I watched Mom slide down against the door to the floor. She prayed and prayed. Mom never stopped praying.

One night after a long night of singing, clapping, and praising God, me, Mom, Sarah, and Curly Sue came home especially happy. We were still singing *"This Little Light of Mine"* as we walked in the door, home from the church. We stayed up that night, laughing and talking like we used to do. Sarah acted like she had forgotten how mean I had been to her and played with me and Curly Sue. Curly Sue had just started taking her first steps. "Getting out of the way for the next baby," the old ladies at the church would say. So Sarah, who had just turned five, stood on one side with me a few feet away calling Curly Sue to walk to us. Mom prepared dinner, and for the first time in a long time, things felt promising.

"Okay, she has had enough," Mom said from the kitchen. Curly Sue had started coughing, a loud, hard cough. Mom came out from the kitchen. "I'm going to lay her down for the night. Sasha, you and Sarah get ready for bed."

Sleep came easy that night. I dreamed a beautiful dream about Sadie. We were running in a field of tall green grass and purple flowers. The sun was a magnificent orange.

We ran, skipped, jumped until we were both exhausted. We sat on a yellow quilt in the grass, and there was a large spread of sandwiches, jam and fruit. Everything tasted like rainbows.

"Thank you for all of this, Sadie."

"Sasha, I did all of this because I need you to be strong. You have been doing a better job of fighting the darkness, but a test is coming. Be strong, Sasha. Be strong."

I woke up to the sound of sirens and screaming.

"Save my baby, save my baby!" I heard Mom screaming over and over. I looked to the left of me and saw Sarah was still sleeping. Oh, thank God she was safe.

Oh, no! Curly Sue! I got up from my pallet and went running to the front door. "What's wrong with my sister?" I yelled at the paramedics.

"Go back inside," was all I got from them.

I saw Mom getting in the back of the truck. "Sasha, stay here with Sarah. When your dad comes back, tell him I'm at the hospital and to get here quick."

What? Wait! When Dad comes back? We haven't seen him in a week. Before I could speak my thoughts, the door to the ambulance shut, and I was left alone standing in the middle of the street.

The days blended together. I did my best to keep Sarah occupied and her mind off Mom and Curly Sue. We spent a lot of time in the backyard at the lake. I took her to church on Wednesday. That turned out not to be a good idea. Too many questions about where Mom was.

Just when food started to become a major issue, Dad came home. He walked into the front door without so much as a hello and headed straight for the bed, where he plopped down with all of clothes on and slept for another two days.

Sarah and I survived off plain dry cornflakes and oranges from the neighborhood trees. I tried all sorts of things to wake Dad. I hadn't seen Mom and Curly Sue now for days. I had too many questions that I needed answered.

I played the TV too loud. I banged empty pots on the counters. Sarah and I jumped on the bed. I cried, Sarah cried, all to no avail.

He woke, unprovoked, one day. Sarah and I were in the room halfheartedly playing I Declare War on the bedroom floor.

"Hey Sasha, hey Sarah, how my babies doing?"

Surprisingly, Sarah didn't do her normal song and dance whenever Dad came around. She sat there pretending to be interested in our card game.

"Dad," I said, keeping my eyes on the cards. "Mom left in an ambulance days ago with Curly Sue. They have been at the hospital, and we don't know anything else. Me and Sarah are hungry. We have been waiting for you to come ever since Mom left."

"Sasha, you are just as dramatic as your mother. If you were so hungry, why didn't you wake me up? Come on, get your sister ready. Let's go make some money to get food and go find out what foolishness your mother has going on."

Dad took Sarah and me around town looking into trash cans collecting soda cans. He had a large black trash bag to collect the cans. He told me we could earn five cents for each can we collected, so we needed to get each one or we would be out here all night.

After hours of digging through trash cans, Dad said, to himself, I'm sure, "Man, fuck this. I got to get some real money if I'm going to get what I need and get these kids something to eat."

Dad drove us to a part of town I hadn't seen before. There were mini mansions everywhere you looked. *He couldn't know anyone who lives here,* I thought.

"Sasha." Dad turned to me in the car and asked, "If you had a way to do something illegal to feed your family, would you do it?"

I looked down and thought about the teachings at church. I looked back at Sarah sleeping on the cracked, duct-taped upholstery. I thought of Mom and Curly Sue, wherever they were. I thought of the empty feeling in the pit of my stomach, and I looked Dad in the eyes and said, "Hell, yes."

"I thought so," he replied as we pulled into a new construction housing project. Dad pulled some tools from the trunk of the car. "Leave Sarah there; she will be fine. Let's go."

Dad turned on his flashlight and started looking for something I didn't know. "The problem with your mom, Sasha, is that she is too uptight, especially since she started going to church. She is too hard on a man, asking for too much and not really understanding. I mean, you understand. You understand that I have to do what I have to do to make money to keep a roof over y'all heads and the lights on. If your mom knew what I was doing, she would have a fit. Matter of fact, don't say a word about what you see. Understand?"

"Yes, Dad." I didn't understand what Dad was doing, so I wasn't going to be able to tell anyone.

I didn't understand what we had done until we got to the junkyard. The man in the booth wanted to know if the copper was stolen. "Nah, man, it's not stolen. Ask my daughter. She will tell you. Do you think I'd go stealing copper with my little girls in the car?"

The man peered over at me. "Alright, man, I'll do it this time. But next time, don't bring this shit to me." I watched as Dad started to unload all the copper onto the scale. The man told Dad he would give him two dollars a pound. When Dad finally put every last piece of copper on the scale, we had a grand total of ten pounds. I watched him meticulously count every last soda can. There were thirty-four. The angry man handed Dad twenty-two dollars and told him never to come back. Dad looked like he had won the lottery. I was sick.

Dad happily jumped back into the car and took us to 7-Eleven. He told us we could get a meal. A hot dog, chips and drink for all our hard work. After I inhaled the hot dog, I was able to worry about Mom again. I asked Dad to take us to the hospital.

"We will Sasha, soon enough. I have a stop I need to make."

It was late, and the sun had already gone down. Where Dad had to go besides the hospital, I couldn't imagine. For the second time that day, Dad took us to a side of town I hadn't ever visited. The difference was night and day. There were people standing on corners and in front of little hut-like houses. Cats and dogs ran the streets. There were half-naked kids with bats chasing land crabs. I rolled up my window and locked the door. I heard Dad laugh and mumble, "Just like your mother."

Dad pulled down a long dark alley. "You and Sarah stay in the car, and I'll be back," he said without looking at me. Sarah started to cry from the back seat. I locked his door and climbed in the back seat with her. The sheet Dad had used to drag the scrap metal laid balled up on the floor of the car. I shook it out as best I could inside the car and covered us as we curled up in the backseat. I sang "*This Little Light of Mine*" until we eventually dozed off.

"Sasha, open the damn door," Dad yelled while he banged on the window.

It was morning, and Dad was just getting back. I unlocked his door.

"Why did you lock the door?" he asked, and I did not respond. Dad backed us out of the alley and asked, "Where to next?"

"The hospital," I whispered, trying desperately to suppress my anger.

"Yeah, we will get to that, no rush. There is this nice park I want to take you and your sister to first."

Families came, and families went. After long hours at the park I was pushed past all levels of frustration. Sarah and I had swung our last swing. The monkey bars had been climbed, and the merry-go-round had gone around enough. I was hide-and-seeked out. Even the fire ants grew tired of biting our legs. We frequented the car begging Dad to wake. We cried out in hunger.

It's hard to pinpoint when the darkness set in. I remember hearing Sadie say, "Fight it, Sasha," just before I balled my fist and punched Sarah until she bled. I punched her over and over. I punched her because I missed Mom and was worried sick about Curly Sue. I punched her because I was hungry, and she was hungry, and there was nothing I could do about it. I punched her because at that moment I hated Dad more than anyone or anything on the planet. I punched her because I couldn't think of anything else to do.

A man in a police uniform finally pulled me off of Sarah. I came out of my trance and saw what I had done to my sister. "Send an ambulance," I heard the cop say into his microphone. He pushed me on the ground, farther away from Sarah.

"Who are you here with, little girl? Where are your parents?"

I looked over at Sarah. She was bloody, dirty, covered in grass and curled up in a ball. She was not moving, and her face was swelling fast. Out of nowhere, Dad appeared.

Looking down at the ground, he stuttered, "What's going on here?"

I got up and tried to attack him. "What's going on is that you are the worst father of all time. We have been here at the park all damn day. We are hungry, and we need to go see Mom."

Dad cowered, and the officer kept me from hitting Dad.

"Sir, is everything okay with you?"

Dad just kept looking down. The medics arrived and started to work on Sarah.

"Sir, is everything okay with you?"

Dad began to mumble and stumble, "Everything is okay. I was just a little tired. I am okay now. Please, sir, I don't want any trouble. Sasha is sorry. She is going through something right now, but she's sorry. Tell the officer you are sorry."

I looked at Dad, and at that moment he was no longer my dad.

The medics told the officer that Sarah needed to be transported to the hospital for further evaluation. *Oh, thank God. The hospital at last.*

Sarah rode in the ambulance. Father and I followed behind in loud angry silence. Once we arrived at the hospital. I took off running looking for Mom. I spotted her in the waiting area. Her hair was standing wild on top of her head. She was still wearing her pajamas from last week. Her eyes were bloodshot.

"Mom!" I screamed.

It took her several seconds to respond. "Sasha! where have you been? I thought I told you to come to the hospital as soon as your father arrived."

"Oh, Mom," I began. "You won't believe where he had us."

"Where is Sarah? Where is your father?"

A medical staff member walked in the waiting area. "Ma'am, there you are. Your daughter has a concussion. We need to keep an eye on her for a few days."

"What? A concussion? How is that possible?"

"Mom, I lost my temper at the park. I beat Sarah pretty bad."

Mom stared at me like I was a stranger. She slapped me with all the force she could muster. I stared back at her.

"You don't know what we have been through," I said through clenched teeth.

She slapped me again and said, "You think you been through something? You haven't been through shit yet."

Father came around the corner. "Curly Sue is going to die," she barked at us and stormed from the waiting room.

Father cried the entire ride home. I was in disbelief. Too hurt to cry. All of the feelings I felt earlier were gone, including the hunger pains. I was numb.

As we entered the house, Father laid on the bed. I started to lay down on the pallet when he asked in a tearful voice for me to lay down with him. Feeling emotionally raw and needing to feel an ounce of comfort, I got in the bed with all my clothes on.

My father tossed and turned, crying out for God to save his baby girl. I laid there unable to feel anything. At some point, I drifted off into a dreamless sleep.

I woke up to the feeling of a rough, dry, large hand under my shirt. I couldn't move. He moved his hand from rubbing my developing breasts, up to my unkempt hair then back down to my breasts.

"I'm so sorry, honey" he said over and over. Did he think I was Mom? I laid there trying not to breathe, trying not to be there. He started to undo my jeans, and my mind drifted to the naked baby doll in Mrs. Brown's desk.

"What the hell are you doing?" I heard Mom say.

Father and I jumped off the bed.

"Sasha, put your shoes on. We are leaving this godforsaken place, and we are never coming back."

Father grabbed Mom by the hand. "I didn't mean anything by it. I was hurt and you weren't here."

"Oh, yeah," Mom said. "Get ready to spend a lot of time alone, 'cause I'm never coming back. We have played the fool for you long enough."

"I love you," Father said despairingly.

Mom snatched her hand away from him.

"We don't love your love," Mom said with finality.

Mom grabbed me by the hand and rushed me outside to the cab that was waiting for us. Through her tears and sobs, Mom explained that the doctors thought Curly Sue had a form of cancer. She said that the hospital was going to medivac Curly Sue to the nearest children's hospital, and Sarah would come, too.

Oh, God. What had I done? I wasn't able to fight the darkness, and now my sisters had to pay the ultimate price, just like Sadie. As we flew, I got real serious with God, and hoped that Sadie was listening, too.

"Dear Heavenly Father,

I come humbly to you asking you to heal my family. I have made a lot of mistakes, but I am sorry. God, I promise to stop bullying if you would just save Curly Sue. I promise to never lay a mean hand on Sarah ever again. I am so sorry for what I did to Sadie. I promise to forgive my father, too. I know that he just needs help for his addiction. I will forgive because I hope that one day, you will forgive me. I am sorry for the lies I told. I can't take them back, but I can try to make things right, right here, right now. I don't want to live like this anymore. The consequences of my actions are too tough to pay. I heard them in church say that with You, old things can pass away, and I can become new. I want to be new. Brand new. Please, God. Please, God. God, please. Amen."

With tears rolling down my face, I heard Sadie whisper, "Good job, Sasha."

Until the next chapter of my life...

Bullying is a major problem throughout the world. We see it everywhere, from schools, work, sports, online and in homes.

My prayer is that by reading my story, you will learn from my mistakes and choose to make better choices. Remember, there are consequences for your actions.

I have attached a pledge to stop bullying in every paperback copy of *It Takes A Fool*. Simply sign the pledge and mail it in. $1 will be donated to the Stop Bullying Now foundation.

If you are a bully or a victim of bullying, please visit www.ittakesafool.com/resources.

Forgive, Congratulate, Laugh, Support, Motivate, Listen. Above all else, Love. It covers a multitude of sins.
- 1 Peter 4:8

Will you sign the pledge?
Together we can end bullying!

I _____ agree to join together to end bullying.

I believe that everybody should enjoy school or work equally, and also enjoy a peaceful life at home and while on the Internet, and feel safe, secure, and accepted regardless of color, race, gender, popularity, athletic ability, disease/disability, intelligence, religion, or nationality.

Bullying can be pushing, shoving, hitting, and spitting, as well as name calling, picking on, making fun of, laughing at, or excluding someone. "Cyber bullying" is when someone is tormented, threatened, harassed, humiliated, embarrassed or otherwise targeted by another person using the Internet, interactive and digital technologies, or mobile phones. Bullying and cyber bullying cause pain and stress to victims and is never justified or excusable as "kids being kids," "just teasing," or any other rationalization. The victim is never responsible for being a target of bullying or cyber bullying.

By signing this pledge, I agree to:
- Value student differences and treat others with respect.
- Not become involved in bullying or cyber bullying incidents or be a bully or cyberbully.
- Be aware of the school's and work policies and support the system with regard to bullying/cyber bullying.
- Report honestly and immediately all incidents of bullying/cyber bullying to a faculty member or supervisor.
- Be alert in places where there is potential for harm, such as bathrooms, corridors, and stairwells.
- Support others who have been or are subjected to bullying/cyber bullying.
- Talk to teachers, parents and adults about concerns and issues regarding bullying/cyber bullying.
- Speak out if I am the victim of bullying or witness bullying in any environment.

Signed by: _____

Print name: _____

Date: _____

Please send your completed pledge to:
Sasha Dreams, P.O. Box 29452, Washington, D.C. 20017

Made in the USA
Charleston, SC
01 December 2014